THE RUNWAY RUNAWAY

THE RUNWAY RUNAWAY

WILLIAN LIMA

Creating Forward Press

Contents

Dear Morgan Jackson,

Thank you for your wisdom and friendship. For your endless support, laughter, and celebrations of life with me - whether in Brazil, the U.S., or 'Do-Buy' Dubai - I dedicate this memoir to you.

With gratitude, brotherhood, and love,
Willian

FOREWARD

As you embark on Willian's journey, I must forewarn you of its shadows. While rich and remarkable, his story bears the dark truths of child abuse and abject poverty - how they weave a pattern through life until a single thread is pulled and the entire story unravels. Since the body remembers abuse, often in the form of PTSD, it takes a determined spirit and a rebirth of body, mind, and soul to navigate the complexities and break free from the shackles of a wretched human condition. As you turn each page, may you do so with a compassionate heart, knowing that Willian overcame crushing deprivation, freeing himself and several family members through persistence, faith, and following the breadcrumbs God laid before him.

Michelle Faith Lucas

1

Better the Devil You Know

"I am taking you home," the woman said, looking down at me with troubled eyes.

"No! No! No! Please, don't take me home. I don't wanna go!"

"Don't worry. I'll be with you. I want to ask your father if I can adopt you."

Even through my dirt and grime, she must have seen my deep, black eyes and straight, dark Indian hair, which strangers had talked about. If she was willing to adopt me, I thought I must have been cute, then she continued, "You can live with me. I'll take care of you and make sure you get a good education."

As a street kid, the hour-long journey to Dad's home was scribbled in my brain. My directions were as impeccable as what would happen at home was predictable.

"Willian, Willian, where have you been?" my brothers asked with a newfound reverent fright when I walked through the door.

But in Dad's eyes, there was no awe. Pure evil lurked in there. His eyes said, "I'm going to kill this kid!" as veins the size of earthworms popped from his neck, and squid-like tentacles flapped across his forehead. I lowered my head to get away from everything on his face.

"Are you this kid's father?" the kind lady asked.

"Yes," Dad replied.

"I found him roaming the streets an hour from here! You're inhumane, and you treat your kids like slaves! Fathers are supposed to take care of their kids!"

"I treat my kids the way I want to! It's none of your business!"

"I work for the Justice Department and can take your kids anytime I want. Willian gets to decide if he comes with me or not."

"He's my kid, and he'll stay with me!"

In the middle of all that yelling, my prayers changed. They'd always been something like, "God, please kill Daddy. If Daddy's dead, me and my brothers and sisters will be okay. My brothers and I will work really hard on the streets. So, God, please kill Daddy." But now I prayed, "God, what am I supposed to do? I want out of this violence, but I don't want to leave my family. Give me a sign, God. Please give me a sign."

"Willian, would you like to come and live with me?" the lady asked, interrupting my pleas.

Daddy got increasingly aggressive. Then the sign came. The worms burst, one after another, and one seemed to clear and break the skin. Red scorpions seemed to dart from his eyes. "Don't dare say yes!" Dad's look exclaimed.

"No. I want to stay with my father," I replied.

"Are you sure you'll be okay?"

"Yes," I lied.

With dagger eyes straight through Dad's soul, the lady declared, "If I hear one whisper that you hurt him again, not only will I take Will, but I'll take all your kids! You'll never see them again. You better watch yourself!"

"These are my kids! I'll do what I want. Get the hell out of my house!"

"You'll go to jail and never get out!" the woman screamed while throwing her finger in Daddy's face.

Now, here's a sobering aside: Dad had just been released from jail for making our home a boxing match. My brother and I had been light-weights pummeled by our heavyweight father about five weeks before I first ran away. When the match was over, Dad had thrown us out of the ring and tied us to a tree, where a passerby discovered us naked and called the police. Dad had left us humiliated and bleeding, abandoned by the street. Those next two weeks became Dad's 'Time-Out' as we called his jail sentence. 'Jail Break Day' started our running away.

The government lady hugged me and said, "I will visit you to ensure you're okay."

I painstakingly watched her car disappear as Dad observed impatiently. If you haven't figured out Dad, what he said next will explain. I apologize for the profanity, but I must get Daddy across to you.

"Who do you think you are, mother fucker? Who do you think you are for bringing a stranger to my house? You are a mother fucker!"

I'd been missing a week, and Dad wasn't even drunk. He concluded as he always did when sober, "When I come back, we'll talk better," and headed to the bar.

That's how my first runaway stint ended after a year at Dad's, three weeks after Jail Break. Little did I know it'd be two more years of weekend bloodbaths before I mustered the courage to run away again.

My bright idea to skip town the first time had come from my brother, Wandeir. He had just come home from running far, far away. On Daddy's Jail Break Day, my brother went past the end of our normal trails to some distant land, as remotely as possible for a ten-year-old. Wandeir had lived on the streets for two weeks. Lucky for him, Wandeir received help from a few good Samaritans before our father found him.

Once Daddy got my brother home, Dad screamed, "Never do that to me! You're my son! You will learn to respect me! I'm going out, and when I come back, we'll talk better," and headed to the bar.

"Dad is dangerous. Why did you leave for two weeks, Wandeir?" I had asked, petrified of Dad's return from the saloon.

But my brother told me how awesome it was to be free and that plenty more kids were on the streets. It sounded cool. I thought I might score some food, a few coins, and maybe even a comic book. I'd be a real-life explorer, sleeping under the stars and perhaps even finding other kids to play with.

So, two weeks after Jail Break Day, and once Wandeir's excursion was over, I planned to flee the following day. But before I could, Dad came home, falling down drunk and carrying belts and wires. We screamed and cried as he started on Wandeir. We slipped, weaved, and tried blocking every punch, but none of it worked. No matter how hard the four of us tried playing bodyguards to our knocked-out brother, we were forced to backpedal into corners. In a flash, we were all down-and-out bleeders by a ferociously quick Iron Mike Tyson.

Alcohol was Dad's encourager, persuader, and ringleader. When he returned from the bar every Friday, the bell would sound. Our pint-sized bodies couldn't run and hide. They'd be whipped around with a violent theatrical flair. But even inside the spectacle that was our home, we respected Dad because we always respected our elders.

Dad left for another city the next day, as he did every Monday morning. And again, we were left alone without food or money. I bolted from the house and hit the streets, hoping to find someone who'd help me get farther away than Wandeir did. Wearing only shorts- shirtless, shoeless, and one step away from being in my birthday suit- I stopped a man driving an awfully big truck. After a little talking, I convinced this stranger to drive me to the next city.

I lived free for a week, but living rough and under the stars wasn't what I'd imagined. I was petrified, feeling kinda like a chick in a hawk's shadow while camping out in a strange city all by my lonesome. Lost souls were everywhere, wanderers with eyes like cracked glass hung near me in the nighttime silence, sometimes grabbing for the same thing I did to lie on.

During the daytime, I had nothing to sell, so I stretched out my hands, hoping someone would drop some coins. But they didn't. Even though I spotted other street kids, they didn't ask me to join their huddle, and I had no clue where they went for shelter.

I didn't stumble upon comic books, but spotted some newspapers blowing around the streets. I rolled them up to make a makeshift pillow. At first, I stayed tucked away in an alleyway, where my bed was just a layer of dirt and gravel, kinda like a bed of nails.

Then, I discovered something amazing! Stores had these boxes that lit up with moving pictures. But my growling stomach didn't allow me the time to pay much attention. My raw hunger kept me moving and gave me the courage to ask for food.

As cool as my brother snatching a Wolf Fish from under a river log, I asked a café owner, "Can you give me some food?" He looked at me inquisitively. "I'll do anything you need to have food." He gave me a meal. I'd need more food for those who knew how many days ahead, so I asked, "May I work for food? I can do the dishes."

"You can clean the floors and arrange the tables for a meal," the generous man replied.

"Thank you," I said, banking one meal a day for the week I slept outside his restaurant's door.

Then, I let down my guard while searching the streets for more money. "Hey, boy! Hey, boy!" I heard. "What are you doing here? Where are your parents?"

I told the woman I was eight years old and explained a little about Daddy before she drove me home and failed to adopt me. That must have been the Sunday after I ran away because if it had been Monday, Dad would have been gone, and I bet we all would have been adopted out.

2

Heaven Knows Why We Were Sent to Live with Dad

In my little world, Daddy's untoward behavior began when I was four years old. So, I'll start from my beginning, with this earliest memory.

Inside our mud and palm hut, Dad started yelling at Momma. His mouth got so huge that I thought he'd swallow one of those beetles that sounded like army helicopters. But instead, he ran outside to our fire pit- that's probably a kitchen to you- and returned, his voice swelling like a storm. I hoped he'd calm down, but he had that thing he used to cut his meat. He raised it like he would slash the roof, but he brought it down on Momma. Red stuff gushed out of her. Daddy threw his hand up in the air again, then back down on Momma, over and over again. The red stuff was everywhere, not just on his meat cutter, but on the dirt floor and even on our hammocks.

At first, Momma was screaming, just like my brothers and sisters. But at some point, while my siblings were still hollering their lungs out, Momma stopped fighting back. It knocked the stuffing out of me to see so much violence, and what I learned was blood. Then, Momma was gone, and we were left with Dad and those sharp things in the pit.

Willian's Family and Home

My mind is blank of memories of those weeks ahead, but I'm sure I relied on my siblings for any semblance of safety. And then, suddenly, Momma came home. It blew my mind that she survived. I don't know how; maybe my sisters prayed. All I know is that when Momma got out of the hospital, we left Goiânia, Brazil, and headed to our grandparents' countryside farm, and there was no more Daddy in our lives-for a while.

Momma said Grandpa responded to our surprise arrival with, "I cannot afford this! There are too many people!" But, because of his loving heart, he gave in and said, "We'll do the best we can."

At our new home, food was limited, and life was risky. We had more space, but our limitations remained the same. We lacked running water, electricity, and any sort of 1980s technology, such as a gas stove that I know about today; a shower was a dump of cold water over the head. That water came from digging holes in the ground. Like pock marks on a quilt, the Brazilian countryside is dotted with those holes. The old plantation house was broken, crumbling outside, and rotting inside. It looked like it might fall apart any minute, especially the stairs. But I didn't care; it was home, just one that showed how tough life was for us in the Brazilian Indian community.

Outside was this magical sea of green adventure for our pigs and chickens. But where crops once stretched as far as the eye could see before I was born, weeds and empty plots took much of the space when I was a kid. With our limited provisions, I plowed that land with Grandpa, helping him plant corn, yucca, and potatoes. Living hand to mouth, everything came from the field. Some days, we ate chicken and sometimes pork, but we never had breakfast or dinner. We'd have one meal a day if we were lucky enough to have food.

That was Mom's humble childhood home, where she worked the fields and missed out on getting an education. She never learned to read or write and would always need someone to help her survive. So, when she was fourteen and met the man who would become my father, eleven years her senior, she moved in with him and started the marriage process.

Here's a side note: Daddy could barely read or write himself, because he had dropped out of elementary school. Mom needed someone to protect her, and since Daddy worked construction gigs, she thought he'd give her a little more than the farm ever could. But although Daddy sometimes built homes and sometimes restored roofs, the word 'sometimes' didn't factor into his drinking.

When I lived on the big farm, my Indian Grandma was blind, and my Cigano Grandpa cared for her. Ciganos are descendants of Romani gypsies who came from Portugal a long time ago when Portugal told them to leave or go to jail. Many Romanis had long time-outs. But, somehow, my relatives made it to Brazil.

People don't see Ciganos much because they're poor, and some folks think bad things about them, like they're fortune tellers and thieves. But my Grandpa wasn't like that at all. He was strong and had a loving soul. And, with Grandma being so gentle, I didn't mind things being so hard. But I desperately wanted food. And more than desperately, I hankered to provide for my family. That became my primary goal at this young age while living on the farm.

School would be the only way to lift my family out of destitution. I had to get educated to get a good job and make good money. So, I walked to school when I could and learned to read and write by seven. I loved learning, and school provided a meal, so that made sure I ate at least once a day. But my siblings and I couldn't go if the family was hungry. "How will we get food?" was the common burning question, and staying home to harvest came first.

Naturally, being a horde of truants, government officials sometimes visited our farm to persuade us to attend school, but they couldn't force us. Daddy was part Black, but we kids were mostly Indian, and everyone knew the unspoken rule: Indian kids were not raised to chase education. We were raised to survive.

Well, you know, things got really tough for us. We didn't have much grub, and I didn't get to go to school often like other kids. So, when I was seven, I started selling ice cream on a stick and veggies on the streets of a nearby town. I made a few coins, but it was never enough to feed everyone in my family.

Struggles got more brutal. Then, Mom had to do something unfortunate- find other people to care for us kids. But nobody would take all five of us, so she split us up. I was lucky because I got to stay with my teenage aunt on the farm next door. I still had to take those chilly showers, but I got used to them because I didn't know any better. But I still have no idea where Valdenir- my sister, six years my senior, Josemir- my brother, five years ahead, Irani- my sis, four years my senior, or Wandeir, who was one and a half years older than me, went.

While we were gone, Momma fell in love. She needed that man; I understood that. Mom wouldn't go hungry and wouldn't have to work so hard with him by her side. Since he could read and write, her new husband would help her in areas that she didn't have a chicken's chance in a jaguar's mouth of handling on her own.

But there was a huge downside for us. Momma's new husband already had three children and couldn't support more kids. As Mom moved away with him, we were wrangled together and sent on a five-hour bus journey to live with our father.

3

If Money Is the Root of Evil, Why Was Daddy Broke?

Moving in with Dad, we had two radioactive disasters. The first was Daddy himself. The second was the Cesium-137 mass contamination of Goiânia, which was started by two men who found a strange container in an abandoned building while looking for scrap to steal and sell. The glowing blue powder inside was thrown around so much like glitter that the government tested 112,000 people for contamination.

It seeped into the water and ground. Some say the radioactive Cesium-137 stays around for a couple of hundred years, and our incident was a bit like the Chernobyl tragedy. It ended up officially killing four people, contaminating around two hundred and fifty, and leaving dozens with radiation poisoning. It was found in homes, buses, and cars, and they even say on 50,000 rolls of toilet paper.

In hindsight, with all of the health issues my family later had, I have to wonder if it wasn't in our river. I'm curious about the unofficial truth, but I don't think the radiation made it into Daddy's liquors.

Alcohol summoned Daddy's ballistic demon when he saw us kids because we reminded him of Mom, and that she divorced him. If I had had the word 'loser' in my vocabulary, and if I hadn't respected Dad, that's the word I would have used to describe him. Life was a nightmare when he was home every Friday night through Monday morning. He was always drunk, frustrated, and violent.

Here's an interjection: At the end of this book, you'll learn that Dad's been demon-free for four years and is the only one of us still living in abject poverty- by choice.

We were ages seven through thirteen when we got this new lifestyle where Dad would work in another city, and we'd be home alone on weekdays. We were left void of food or money, but had the river, our everything. It was our laundry room, bathtub, kitchen sink, and food cabinet. If our clothes were dirty, we could scrub them against the smooth stones that lined the river's bank, but that was a rarity because the only clothes we had were on our backs. We could bathe in the river, but we were too focused on finding food to care that dust clung to our scalps and grime covered our skin. We cleaned our dishes in the river on the blessed days that we'd actually catch a few small fish.

At eight years of age, I worked the streets full-time. Wandeir and I teamed up. He scavenged and sold trinkets while I used supplies from Daddy's house to shine shoes. My shoe-shining business began making the best money of all! I was so excited to put a bit of food in our mouths, but my first bout of depression began because I had to miss school, as did my siblings.

Still, I became tough. When a potential customer said 'no,' I didn't give up. I'd go to the next person and then the next person. If that didn't work, I'd beg a little, as did my siblings. We'd hit every bar, hoping a drunk would be so loose that they'd give us some change. A few did. Most yelled, "Get the hell out of here!"

Carmo do Rio Verde was a small town, and people didn't have money. The streets were broken, dusty, and muddy, just like us. The bars were modest, not possessing a lick of charm, and filled with drunkards, just like Daddy. I got used to that type of person very quickly and decided that not only would I never be like them, but I'd make myself into a dignified person. I didn't want to be a loser. I yearned to know what dignity felt like.

The stores were small, but I hungered to buy something in them, like one of the tempting treats they had stacked in their windows. I'd stop before them and watch motorbikes go by, hoping one would park, and I'd score a few coins by ensuring it didn't get stolen. "Can I watch this for you so no one will steal it?" I'd ask. They usually thought I was a thief and shooed me away.

Most of those town-dwellers seemed evil, but a few were saints, like the man who gave me a container to put my shoe-shining supplies in and carry on my back. That made my days more manageable and made me look more professional and proper. It helped me get clients and gain a little more money. I'll always have deep gratitude for that man. I also have a great appreciation for one saint lady who often invited me into her home for milk and cookies because she knew I was starving.

Yet, with five mouths to feed, I painstakingly searched for more jobs. I cleaned people's yards, washed cars, and ran errands when someone would hire me. But whatever I was doing, I lived in abject terror of Dad arriving home on Friday evenings. As soon as he'd walk through the door, he'd say, "I'm going to the bar, and when I return, we'll talk better." He'd return three sheets to the wind and commence floggings that he called spankings. The four of us spent Friday evenings bleeding on the floor. I say four of us because Irani was never in the mix. When I was a baby, she was injured in an 'accident' that left her with severe burns on her front side. Dad spared her.

Neighbors did nothing when they heard our screams until the naked tree incident. On that horrific day, the same electrical wires Dad used on our skin, he used to tie us up. Everything bled, even our mouths and eyes. Passersby had the same look of terror my siblings and I had for a year. "What's going on?" one asked before yelling for help from authorities. Dad's jabs were far from legal, and showcasing us added insult to injury. We were utterly degraded, our cheeks burning with embarrassment. Little did I know that humiliation would become my life trend for almost two decades.

The police came, untied us, helped us dress, and took us away as Daddy was being taken to lock up. Valdenir came to the station with salt to clean our wounds, which she'd always used. The very painful concoction of salt and water was all we had for healing, and since our injuries didn't appear internal, no one would take us to a hospital. Neighbors pleaded with the authorities to get us into a shelter, but even from jail, Dad imposed his power. "They will stay together at their home!"

The police told Dad on Jail Break Day, "If you do anything like this again, you'll go to jail longer, and we'll adopt your kids out."

Instead, Wandeir ran away when Dad returned, exclaiming, "I'm never going to drink again. I'll be better. I love you and won't beat you again." We knew that was pure crap talk, and Wandeir gathered the guts to bolt.

We didn't inform our mother of her runaway kids or of her abusive ex-husband going to jail. How could we? We didn't have a telephone or the money to put a letter in the mail.

Here's an afterthought: If money creates evil, and evil created Dad's wicked behavior, then why was Daddy broke?

4

Whose Cross Was It to Bear?

I dreamed of Mom while crying every day after I was returned home by the kind lady. I missed Momma and dearly wanted to live with her, but Valdenir said Momma's husband wouldn't have it. We did our best to live with Dad and inside his wreckage of a home.

Interestingly, in a life wrecked by trauma, I didn't expect the worst day of my nine years to come from Valdenir, my caretaker sister. She was my guardian and the only sister I had left in the house. Daddy had recently farmed out Irani to a farming family who treated her like a slave. She did all their housework, including caring for the babies, in exchange for a bed. She never got a penny.

Right before Valdenir laid it on me, Dad disgraced her with a beating in front of her friends. He had just grabbed her from her friend's party, pulling her by her hair, hitting her with a tire rubber, and then ripping her clothes in the middle of the street.

"I'm leaving to live with Mom, Willian. I'll try to get you a bus ticket so you can come to live with us."

She was my protector and salt nurse. She was the only savior in my universe. I watched her leave from the bus station while my stomach turned and tore, my eyes streaming with tears. I hadn't known that such pain existed. I thought, "Now it's only me and my brothers. How will we survive?"

I kept working, and my little container was now my everything. It held my world; it contained my only means of survival. Some days, I could buy a banana or a candy bar with the money I earned. On one especially starving day when no fish were in our river, I went to a gas station to find work. I asked the only employee there, "Do you want me to clean your shoes?"

"No," he replied, "but you can do other things to make extra money."

"What can I do? I'll do anything!"

"Well, we can go to that room over there, and you can help me with stuff. Do you want to find out what it is?"

"Sure, let's go," I happily replied, thinking I'd be cleaning or organizing boxes.

Within moments, the man stripped his clothes off and grabbed me. "No! No!" I screamed.

"The door is locked. There is no way to escape. I will pay you to do what I say," he whispered. I shouted, but the street was too noisy for anyone to hear. "If you scream, I'll spank you." Intense fear stopped me from shrieking.

"Please open the door, please," I begged.

"No. You're not leaving until you give me what I want."

I prayed, "God, help. What do I do?" I felt God was saying to pretend I'd give him what he wanted. "Just pretend, Willian," was the message I received through a feeling.

Here's a footnote: I had an acute awareness that it was my first time seeing a naked adult. My nine-year-old eyes couldn't believe the hairy, mature thing they saw, and I couldn't comprehend what the man was doing with it!

I did as God said, which relaxed the beast. The man tried raping me for what felt like ten minutes before I pleaded, "Please don't hurt me. I'll do whatever you want."

I don't know what he was doing the next moment, but I knew he was vulnerable. I grabbed my container, raised it high to the sky, and brought it down, whacking him over the head. I grabbed the door knob, and the door opened. I had no idea how I'd just escaped, but I ran and ran and ran without looking back and without my container.

"Thank you, God."

"I'm glad you listened, son."

5

To Hooker Hell and Gone

Bowing to the floor, hands clasped, I continued praying, "God, please get us bus tickets to Momma's. Please let me live with her. If you can not do that, please kill Daddy."

I dearly missed Mom and dreamt of her wide open arms and glowing smile when she would finally see me standing at her door. I imagined myself not being a loser and having a new container with fancy supplies that got shoes sparkling clean. I wanted to work the streets of Momma's town and get good gigs there, cleaning every yard in the town. I fantasized that I lived with Mom and paid for everything in the house. Shoot, I could make so much money that I'd buy us a new house. And with all that cash, I'd buy bus tickets for my brothers. I wasn't just going to get me and Momma out of deprivation; I was determined to lift my entire family up and away on a giant magic carpet.

But, as my brothers and I aged, we got filthier, our clothes got more ragged, and our feet began resembling chipped paint. Whatever the cause of our increased destitution, muck didn't help business. Then, my pocket bank account was busted at age ten, making me realize I desperately needed to return to school. I yearned to study hard and get a big job that people landed when they graduated from high school. I hadn't been to school for three years. I was stuck in the hostility of the streets. Sometimes, I made a few coins or found discarded clothing, but most of the time, I was chased away from potential customers.

Although I worked hard, cleaning anything an owner would allow me to, there was a bright light. I was introduced to cartoons. I'd found homes with kids and glowing boxes, which I learned were TVs. When parents opened their doors or windows to let fresh air in, I'd cautiously sneak to their yard and peek inside at the flickering glow. The colorful images and characters dancing across the screens made the temptation too strong to resist. I'd be pulled into the enchantment and jokes for a few minutes, but the homeowners always caught me. They'd come to the door or window, their faces contorted with disgust, and slam it shut in my face. The rejection felt like a slap across the cheek, and I was left with a heavy heart of disappointment.

So, I came up with another way to watch cartoons. I saved every coin I had to buy one of those boxes, putting my needs for food aside. I got a used black and white TV and took it home. But, it was so hard to see that my brothers and I had to drape ourselves and the TV with a black cloth and scoot up real close. That lasted three weeks before it turned to jittery squiggles, lapsing into a tiny white light and poof, died.

Then, suddenly, my life was like my TV screen. My whole world was flipped upside down while lights flickered on and off. The whole lot of us bolted to the bus station. It must have been a weekday when our father was gone. I don't recall how it happened or why my brothers and I left. That memory is black for me, probably due to fear. It's likely from my terror of what Daddy would do. The thought of him catching us must have put me in a trance that later translated to some sorta amnesia.

Now, here's an addendum: I didn't tell you what Dad did to me the night I returned from my first runaway attempt. It would have been too much, and you'd probably stop reading. That detail created a horror that gripped my soul like a vice. The three of us running away  from Daddy will permanently reside in the shadows of my mind. However, I bet Valdenir had something to do with those bus tickets.

We fled the nausea of embarrassment, the stomach knots of dreading Dad's return, the beatings, and the crushing weight of humiliation. During the ride, I daydreamed about being a happy family again and getting a meal at school. I longed to be in my mom's arms and hugged by my salt nurse.

But when we arrived, Mom held a toddler girl in one arm and reached out the other for a one-arm embrace. We relished her kisses, but then her husband said, "I can't care for these kids in this tiny house. You're my wife, and you need to take care of my kids!" So, we were relocated to different families, and I was again living with my young, impoverished plantation aunt, who now had two small kids.

Things weren't all so bad. I headed to school- my elevator out of poverty. I received a white shirt and navy blue shorts as a uniform. It became my wardrobe and my first spotless attire. Teachers donated a few items, like used clothing, flip-flops, and shoes a size too small. I felt good in my new clothes and clean for the first time in years.

I was initially proud, although I winced, shuffling through the hallways. I walked so awkwardly that I filled my shoes with water to stretch them. That didn't work out so well.

I had to provide for my aunt and her family, since I was a burden to a family who could barely feed themselves. I looked for work every day after school. Quickly, I was cleaning yards, washing cars, and doing farm work. But this gave my uniform a very short life, and my clothes were rapidly back to ratty.

We didn't have the means to patch the holes, so my pride quickly turned to shame. My garments, grimy skin, skeletal, scraggly body, and bizarre walk appealed to the bullies. "Willian is so ugly!" they'd scream in my face. "Hey, you filthy, bony bastard!" some said, trying to get me to fight. Yeah, my hair was matted, and dirt clung to every crevice on my body like Earth herself was my uniform. But I once was almost adopted, and maybe there was a sliver of a chance that something cute hid underneath.

I tried keeping good thoughts in my mind, because in some odd way, I'd learned something spectacular on the streets: The better my thoughts, the more customers I'd get. The more hopeful my thoughts were, the happier my days would be.

Regardless of my good thoughts at school, the yelling would ensue. "There goes nitty, gritty Willy!" Kids much larger than I would come charging, eager to yank and tear at my uniform, leaving it in tatters. It was a rude awakening, hitting me like a water balloon. I was ugly, emaciated, and clueless as to why that nice woman had wanted me. But, I could not dwell on that because school was ultra-important. It would lift me out of the dangers of the streets and impoverished farm life.

Yet, as the taunting got harsher, the more it dawned on me that the school I craved wasn't safe. It was just safer than living with Daddy. I had to run somewhere out of harm's way. I was prepared, but I didn't know where.

It's funny how these things happen. But here it goes, this is how I came to discover where my next destination would be:

When I could, I'd visit Mom. Over one visit, I struck up a conversation with a woman in her neighborhood. The woman offered to give me a few coins to do her grocery shopping and clean her yard. I did this several times, and after a few weeks, she said, "I have two ladies moving to another city. One of them is my sister, who has a baby. You can live with them and help with the baby. You'll get fed that way."

I couldn't conceive what she meant by 'having ladies,' but it sounded like a great opportunity! My not-yet-eleven-year-old mind thought, "I don't have anyone to protect me. I've been on my own for a long time." I had to talk with myself because it was the only expert advice I'd get. "I need to do something for myself." So, I told the woman, "I'll go!" and darted away from the plantation and school.

The ladies picked me up from the street, and we took a grueling four-hour bus ride away from Mom. Over the months ahead, I turned eleven, washed dishes, cleaned the house, and cared for the infant. The women would say, "We have clients coming over now. Take the baby to your room. Lock the door, and don't come out until we say."

Then I'd hear them take men into their bedrooms, and soon after, I'd hear the men take them.

It was a relatively easy few months until I was kicked out after one of their repulsive clients showed up when I was alone. "I am a man, and I'm not willing!" I explained. "They'll be home soon!"

"You don't have a choice!" he said, jerking at my clothes.

The childless woman walked through the front door as the man ripped off my shorts. "What are you guys doing?" she screamed.

"Your boy was trying to steal your client to make money," the despicable man replied, blaming me.

Without hesitation, the hooker kicked me out, and I was back on the streets of another strange city. After several days, the lady with the baby found me and tried to get me to return. "I need you," she said.

"No. I want to go to Mom's," I answered. This prompted her to strike me. But finally, I was mature enough to protect myself. I fended her poundings off and returned to those alien streets until I made enough money for a bus ticket and headed back to Mom.

First, I stopped by the Madam's house- not understanding that's what she was, of course- to tell her what her whores did to me. She may have talked with Mom. I don't know because Mom's husband said I could live with them now.

It worked for months, but with my brothers occasionally living there in such a cramped space, fighting between step-siblings spilled over into Mom and my stepfather fighting. I was grateful to have a roof over my head and a little food. I was thankful to one of my step-siblings, Robson, who became like a true blood brother to me.

Since he had green eyes, ivory skin, and bright blond hair, we nicknamed him 'Grandfather,' which in Portuguese is 'VoVô.' But our living arrangements hurt Mom, and I had to do something about that. I was almost twelve, and I had to get my life organized! I had to make something of my life. Before disappearing, I hugged my mom, siblings, and VoVô goodbye. As I left, I decided to find God in a small Protestant church across town.

6

My Escape to Limbo

The people at church were dressed up like they had just stepped out of a window display. Women seemed ready to meet angels or something, and the men in their shiny shoes were fit to be kings. Even the kids looked like they were from fairy tales, dressed up like princes and princesses straight out of my cartoons. Boys my age wore suits and ties. The girls wore flowery dresses and black satin shoes. I felt so inadequate and ashamed in my rags and flip-flops, but I hoped people of faith would look past my despicable self.

There were many VoVôs in church, young and old, and a few of them treated me like my VoVô did. Some adults treated me as a son, but others disregarded or humiliated me, seemingly to push me out of their White church. The bullying was less than at school initially; therefore, finding God was safer than learning math. But I still went to school when I could to create a better life and prayed in church that my family would have food. I promised God that if I made good money, I'd throw away my dirty garments, buy fresh church clothes, and help my family escape poverty.

It wasn't long before the bishop approached me and said, "If you take care of the church, you can live in a little room in the back with a small bed." At twelve, I was ready to get my life together by living in that church and having God in my life. So, I left the one person I'd longed to live with for years. I felt I was permanently walking away from Mom, so she and I would have better lives.

Soon, many in the convocation needed my help. They asked that I clean their homes, and I'd do the job and get fed. They'd go on vacation and need someone to watch their homes. I'd get a bed or a couch for some nights and eat from their refrigerators. Some members offered me food every day, whether I was cleaning their home or the church.

I sang in the choir, learned to play guitar, and played during church service. I was moving up in the world. I'd go to one house one day to work and get a meal, and to another home the next day. Yet, many of the young VoVôs increased their laughter at my dreadfulness, dark skin, gaunt body, and revolting face.

A few of the teens were the harshest. It's crazy how such hatefulness can come through youth! However, one beautiful young White woman who glowed like a saint- I'll call her Concella- could be a snob, but I guessed she was allowed to since her skin was so pale and her hair so silky. Still, one Sunday morning after service, while everyone remained behind chatting, she called the only dark kid in the congregation- the one who took church and school seriously, who cleaned the church, performed during service, and wanted to build a good life with God- a 'nigger' and 'monster.' She disgraced me in front of the church, and it's been one of the hardest things for me to forget.

**Here's a curious partial postscript:** Decades later, when I caught sight of that woman again, she had tied the knot with a church member. Together, they had two boys: one fair-skinned and one Black.

The younger bullies got beefier, while I stayed a toothpick, only growing in apprehension of myself. "Look at waddling Willian run away," they'd say when I wore tight shoes that hurt like hell. "You're black like an army ant and walk like a spider! You're hideous!" they'd yell, then run off with their girlfriends.

I wanted a girlfriend, but I wasn't lovable. By thirteen, I noticed how cute some of the church girls were. I wanted to hold hands with one just like the other boys. I wanted someone to love me, but no one would. My depression returned when I realized that everyone in my world saw me as a person who could not be loved.

I studied when I could while living in and caring for that church for nearly two years. But something overtook me. Shame- a disappointment in myself. I was embarrassed for being almost fourteen and still living like I had with Dad- going from person to person, asking for food.

Many teenagers didn't like me because I was ugly and wore scraggly clothes. They made sure I knew that every day. So, I decided to tell the bishop about the bullying, trusting he would take care of one bad aspect of my life. I would take care of the beggar part of me. I had to shift my shame. That was my responsibility.

Instead of hearing what I'd hoped for, the bishop responded, "Members are complaining that you're sleeping in homes instead of the church. We agreed you'd take care of the church. You must stay here and work hard or get out."

I felt like his slave, which made me want to run. I was embarrassed, but where was I to turn? I asked a few church members for help. Although I had good relationships with several adults, none could take me in. So, I dashed back to Mom, hoping I wouldn't be in the way and cause any hurt like the last time.

I discovered a church near Mom's and attended services twice or thrice weekly. I was determined to turn my life around. VoVô and I teamed up, hitting the streets together to hustle and provide for our family. We sold snacks, ran errands, and scavenged for anything we could use at home. Despite our poverty, we found a sense of freedom that brought us closer together, in a bond tighter than blood could bind.

On one of the most significant days of my life, VoVô and I worked on opposite sides of a street selling ice cream. I observed VoVô start to cross the street. A speeding car came from nowhere. The world ground to a halt as VoVô stood frozen in the car's path. Tires screeched, someone screamed, and then there was a mind-numbing thud. I helplessly watched my brother fly across the road as all the air was vacuumed out of my chest. I ran to him. He took a gasping breath. It was his last one, although my thirteen-year-old mind didn't want to believe it and couldn't grasp the enormity of what had just happened.

An ambulance took us to the hospital, where I waited, believing a doctor would save my brother. The sickening crunch reeled in my mind, but I imagined the doctor happily coming to the lobby to tell me VoVô had survived. Instead, the doctor said, "I'm sorry, your brother is dead."

I screamed and cried as I stumbled forward, trembling. My brother being dead was unthinkable. The pain was too much! Then the doctor said, "Go home and tell your family what happened. Tell them your brother is dead." I screamed some more. The thought of relaying such pain to them, telling them that our world just crashed down, especially to VoVô's father, was overwhelming. "I'll have the ambulance take you home, boy," the doctor ended.

I asked the driver to stop when the ambulance was some distance from my stepfather's house. I needed the walk, so I could gather my thoughts and figure out how to tell my family.

All of my traumas suddenly possessed my body as I exited the vehicle. The world seemed to spin vertically like the sky had just sunk beneath my feet, and the gravel covered my head.

I trudged a block with tremors running up and down my spine. The world began to fade. I felt suddenly adrift, and my thoughts wafted away in a wisp of smoke. My brain went black, and I surrendered to the darkness.

The next thing I recall is looking up at Mom and my stepfather blocking the brooding sky and screaming, "What's going on!?" Not a word came out of my mouth. I realized I was lying in the middle of the street. I started bawling. I couldn't say a thing, only sob. "What's going on!? What's going on!? What's going on!?" they repeated.

Finally, I muttered through a mouth drowning in tears, "VoVô had an accident and died."

A chaotic home life persisted for weeks. My stepfather was in deep mourning and didn't like having so many people in the house, so he fought with Mom. He hit her in front of me one day, and it was the first time I felt brave enough to stop a man from hitting anyone. I said, "I'm not going to allow that!"

He punched me, then said, "If you're a man, you can handle it! We can fight man to man!"

I responded, "I respect you. I live in your home, but I don't want to fight."

"Get out!" he yelled, and I headed to my aunt's penurious plantation, visiting Mom when I could.

On one visit, six months after VoVô's death, my stepfather got sick. He said it was his heart. Since Mom was scared of ambulances and hospitals, feeling she couldn't handle them, much less read or understand anything given to her, she asked me to go with my stepfather in the ambulance. He surprised me on the ride when he said, "Willian, I'm sorry about what happened. I was anxious and depressed. I wasn't thinking. I'm sorry. I know I'm not going to return home. I'm going to die in the hospital."

"No, no, no. Don't think that way. You're going to get better."

"I won't get better. I'm terrified." He started to cry.

"You're going to come back. You'll heal and come back home." And those were our last words, although I left him alive with the doctors.

Growing up in such meager conditions, the big world made Mom panicky. She was petrified to go to the hospital the next day and believed her husband would soon return home. So I took her place. When I arrived, a doctor came to the lobby and said, "He died, boy. Go home and tell your mom."

Dread does not describe the aftereffects of that punch in the gut. Telling Mom that her husband died was a devastating thought. With a lifetime of trauma, the last thing we needed was another one. I thought of saying, "I'm sorry, Mom, but he didn't make it. He died." I practiced the entire way home, but my mind went black. Trauma had a way of making everything go dark. Mom had such a rough life; I couldn't make it worse. Who would take care of her? Who would ensure she was fed and had a roof over her head? But there was no avoiding the immediate pain because the doctors said someone needed to get the body.

"M-mom," I stammered, hands trembling and lungs choked by angst. "He didn't make it."

The news washed over her like a tidal wave of coal. She suffocated and shattered into a million irreparable pieces at once. Not only did she love her husband, but he was the only person who provided and cared for her. Then, ragged gasps erupted from her being, which turned into simultaneous sobs and screams. A torrential downpour of tears fell from her eyes. She went outside and walked around the house ten times with her hands on her head, howling, "No! No! No!" her cries echoing through the neighborhood.

I don't know who paid for the mortician who retrieved the body. We certainly did not. Mom suffered wildly for the first two months. For nearly forty-five days, she slept at his grave every night. That remains one of the most heart-wrenching sights I've ever witnessed.

7

Baptism by Fire

When every thread of hope feels frayed and worn, there's a peculiar comfort in the notion that life cannot descend further into darkness. The abyss stared at me as if saying, "There's no hope for you here, Willian." A strange solace wafted through me with an opposite knowing: the only path left is upward.

My family's pain had reached a crescendo, and a defiance in me was born against the relentless onslaught of misfortune. I knew I had another storm to weather, but on the other side, I'd look back at the wreckage that was my life and blow away its ashes.

I was fourteen and providing for myself, my aunt and her family, and now Mom, who had come to live with us on the farm. I continued to sing and play music at church, and school was so spotty that I'd need propulsion to get me out of the darkness.

So, I painstakingly went to Mom and said, "I need to do something with my life. If I keep living here, things will never change." As soon as I set that intention, I learned that I had a paternal aunt in Rio de Janeiro, and I got my head and heart set on running there, hoping she'd take me in. My only hope was to find her address and mail her a letter.

After much effort, I found her address and wrote to her. She responded two weeks later, upon learning that I existed. We kept in touch, and my dream letter came a few months later.

"You can stay with me for a while, Willian. I will support you until you get a job. It isn't safe here for teenagers, though. I live in a ghetto filled with armed gangsters. They sell drugs in my front yard. But, you are welcome here."

My life couldn't get worse, and running wouldn't work this time. Rebellion. I needed to rebel against poverty. I was willing to move twenty-four hours away to unknown Brazilian parts. I wasn't at risk of getting involved with drugs or gangs, as I was committed to a life of dignity.

We never know what we'll get until we try. So, to pay for the journey, I worked on a plantation with Mom. We awoke every day at 3:00 am because the bus hauling the workers left at 4:00 am. We protected ourselves from head to toe to keep mosquitoes, sharp leaves, and the sun at bay. We picked oranges, tomatoes, and peppers, which kept me from school- the one thing I needed to escape deprivation.

After three months of arduous work, I saved a grand-slam total equivalent of thirty dollars. I gave ten to Mom and ten to the bus station for my ticket to Rio. I stuffed the last ten into my pocket to have something when I reached my new home.

At fifteen, I bolted on an excursion I couldn't have dreamt up. Over twenty-two hours on the bus, I counted cars, cows, and clouds until I could no longer. Then, a barely visible skyline of buildings, taller than I'd imagined possible, came into view. A blanket of smog, draping down to a polluted ocean, obscured them and the sun. A multitude of vile bridges stained my mind's eye. Where I once imagined the Atlantic Ocean as glistening blue was replaced by a memory of a dirty ice cream stick falling to the dirt. Never seeing the sea, I hadn't imagined it would be as dreadful as I.

Once in the city, we passed dozens of miles of ghetto favelas, densely packed together and overcrowded, with steep inclines and narrow alleyways. They made our Goiás shanties look like charming cottages. At 5:00 am on January 4, 1996, I arrived at the Rio de Janeiro bus terminal.

Clueless about how to get to my aunt's home, I hung around the station, thinking, "Now what?" As skinny as those peppers I'd been picking, my skin a little darker from the crop work, and my hair a little wavier from aging, I held tight to my ragged suitcase that held a few tatty items and sat for hours.

Once I thought my aunt could be awake, I showed an attendant the address I had scribbled on paper. "Take the little bridge across the street, then take the bus that says 'Bangu' because that is the closest neighborhood to your aunt's home. No bus goes to her neighborhood. It's too dangerous for public services."

At 9:00 am, I got the nerve to take the Bangu bus. We passed through Rio from end to end. For two hours, I was wide-eyed, viewing ghetto after ghetto after ghetto pass by. Leaning homes with tin roofs seemed to be stacked upon one another, climbing hills, cut only by dirt paths crossed by clothes lines and trodden by dogs, winding through hordes of people.

I'd never presumed so many favelas existed. And I couldn't have imagined I'd be living in a favela that was a stronghold of criminal organizations, where violent conflicts often erupted over control of drug trade routes.

My aunt's home was supposedly three or so kilometers from the bus's final stop. Although I cautiously stepped off the bus, I naively walked through the crowds, often stopping people to ask for directions. I was clueless that I was talking with armed gangsters, although shadowy creatures gathered, their faces obscured by bandanas.

The big thing I noticed was their stares, which said, "Who is that weird guy?" This got my heart pounding out of my chest, and when brutish guys began following me, my breath caught in the back of my throat. Still, I continued strolling, glaring straight ahead, until I found my new safe haven that I'd be calling home.

My aunt Lourdes was friendly. After hugs and introductions to her three kids, her husband, Adeir, showed he was sterner and doubtful. He spoke earnestly, saying, "Willian, this is a hazardous area. There's always gunfire and thugs selling drugs at my front gate. You must be careful. Take care of yourself and be careful with your friendships."

I'd never seen drugs in my life. Other than Daddy's hands, the only weapon I'd seen was his meat cutter. I couldn't grasp the dark enormity that I'd just walked into. "I will adapt to the situation," I said to myself.

If I were to cling to the way I thought things should be, I'd be absent from reality. Responding to the here and now is what kept me alive on the streets; it kept me present, which ultimately brought me the saint who gave me the container. By the time I was standing in this life's detour, I knew my container had saved me in two ways. So, I chose to stay awake to the TV show called Life. I couldn't drape a black cloth over my eyes and pretend to see better. I couldn't resist Life, just accept that God was somewhere within it, and move to its beat as the river swept me along.

Holding onto my most hopeful thoughts, I believed school would build me a bridge over rushing waters. There had to be a school nearby, and starting my education again was a priority. Books had not been on my syllabus for a long time. The streets had. I longed to study again. Unfortunately, my aunt couldn't afford another mouth in the house, and I needed to make money so I wouldn't burden her family. As the stream sometimes beats the rocks, work trumped school for what felt like the millionth time.

I feared no one would hire a fifteen-year-old. Yet, a blessing came. Adeir introduced me to his brother, Paulo, who was opening a video store next door and employed me. My aunt brought me food to the store daily, and I took home a little cash for her. I didn't want to be a nuisance, so I ate only one meal daily. But with the bit of money I gave her, she made the meals matter.

With the palpable threat of violence around every street corner, walking to and from work was nerve-wracking. The constant fear of being collateral damage in turf wars or being pounced on as prey for a desperate hoodlum weighed on my soul. I had to continually remind myself that being a video store clerk was my first official job and that I'd taken a giant leap out of the desperation I had lived in.

However, the ghetto violence mentally carved itself into me a year in. I felt like a Cigano amulet, waiting to be sliced and to have something shiny shoved in me. Moreover, living with the daily grief caused by gunfire, I had no choice but to prioritize my education over my aunt's family. So, I went to my aunt for help with finding a school, but she had news for me before I could explain.

Lourdes said, "Willian, Adeir says you should give him your income because he's the man of the family and the provider."

"What?" I asked. "But you get the groceries that feed me."

"He's giving me a hard time, Willian. I don't want any fighting, so please give him your money. I need you to give him your paychecks." I succumbed to her wishes, and there weren't any extras after that.

I wasn't about to let go of my dream of dignity. Education was my only way up and over the ghetto. My aunt later tried to find me a school, but the search was too late; the sign-up period had ended. After another year of selling video games, watching kids playing *Cadillacs and Dinosaurs* and other arcade games, navigating menacing husks of people through a warzone, and dodging bullets, I signed up for school. At age seventeen, I was officially enrolled in elementary school.

Tangent Alert! By the way, a favela is like a city shantytown, and here's an image of the one I lived in as a teenager, so I can make it dramatic for you.

Willian's Favela in Rio de Janeiro

8

Saving Grace

A girl, Elaine, began hanging out at the video store. It was weird. She'd stay close by me, chatter-boxing it up. Sometimes, she acted shy and sometimes high-spirited. Her behavior was puzzling. I assumed she needed a friend or wanted me to introduce her to my cousin. There was no doubt that my body was made for vultures and that I was too unattractive for any girl to take an interest in me.

But underneath the mystery, I had a nagging sense that maybe, just maybe, there was something special about the way she looked at me. My heart began skipping a beat each time she entered the store. So, one day, I leaned casually against the counter, hanging my hand over its side close to her. She grabbed my hand and gave it a tickle. I immediately thought, "I can't even buy her ice cream." Elaine quickly became another reason to better myself.

The ghetto and its gangsters got worse the closer I got to eighteen. Recruiters for drug lords now took to putting guns in my back. They demanded I follow their lead. But Dad had made me come from an ilk of disrepute. I wasn't about to let criminals get me off track. I told them, "I didn't come here for this. I came here for a better life and to help my family," and somehow always escaped.

But then, I was too often in the wrong place at the wrong time. Like the time I came across people who'd been tied to the rails. I was helpless to assist them, and in that second of shock, I watched trains decapitate them.

Then, while distributing flyers for a city council candidate, I heard a car pull up behind me. I turned to see a hoodlum get out of the car and put multiple bullets into a guy, centimeters from me. I thought, "I'm going to die right now!" I was frozen, staring at the car and its criminals.

"What are you looking at? Don't look at us! Don't look at us! Turn and look at the wall!" the dude with the gun screamed. They took off as I moved my eyes toward the ground, seeing a guy riddled with bullets bleeding to death next to me.

My desire for a better life became fiery, and I applied for the Brazilian Army. I explained my situation to the sergeant who interviewed me. "I come from Goiás, where I grew up with little to no food and dangerous living conditions. Now, I live in one of the most deadly favelas in Rio. I think the army is the only way I can have a better life and get out of the ghetto. I want the opportunity to grow through the military."

"I know where the Senador Camará ghetto is," Sergeant Roni replied. "It's close to where I live, but your area is one of the roughest and most dangerous. You would have to take very strenuous exercise tests to ensure you're even capable of joining the army, Willian. That's a challenge because you look too weak to pass. Only the people with the strongest bodies pass the tests."

Sergeant Roni paused for what seemed like forever, took a deep breath, and finally added, "Don't worry. I'll do my best to get you into the army."

By this time, I'd learned that ole' Adeir had a cocaine addiction, and that's where my money was going. I was malnourished and frail because food was scarce. It had been a long time since Aunt Lourdes had been able to give me a meal that mattered.

Passing the army's physical stress tests seemed impossible. How would I get through the first one? Yet, in the beauty of that moment, with the opportunity I was afforded, and hearing Sergeant Roni's support and words, I was elevated. A breath of fresh air lifted me out of a dark sea of impossibility to the possibly achievable. So, I went home, exercised for a few weeks, and returned for my life's most demanding physical test.

Other than not finishing one of the exercises in the set of Physical Readiness Tests, I did pretty well for a feebly scrappy dude. Surprisingly, I passed- barely, because Sergeant Roni ensured it. He told me I was good enough to move on to the following tests.

I ran back to my ghetto home pumped up. My aunt was overjoyed, and I felt proud of myself for the first time in my life. I dreamed of my future army career and helping Mom move to a home of her own. I continued to do well with the tests and with much support from Sergeant Roni.

But when I arrived for my final test, Roni was not there. A Sergeant Alessandro was. As I strode into the testing room, anticipation mingling with nerves, his disdainful gaze met my faithful one. No greeting, just a scowl etched deep into his features as if my presence offended him. His words cut like a blade, slashing through any hope I held.

"Go home," he spat, his voice dripping with contempt. "You're not fit for the army!" And with a forceful kick, he cast me out, extinguishing any flicker of aspiration within me.

I went home bawling. "I didn't make it into the army. That was the only way I'd make something of myself! The good sergeant wasn't there," I cried to Aunt Lourdes. I broke down, heaving with emotional pain of depths I hadn't experienced for years. My depression was back, and I was the gloomiest person in the video store for the next week.

But then, a loud knock came to the door one morning while we were still sleeping. I heard my aunt answer it and then run outside my bedroom.

"Sergeant Roni found you, and he's at the door," she whispered.

I jumped from the bed and ran to Sergeant Roni, who asked, "What are you doing here and not at the base?"

"Sergeant Alessandro kicked me out. I'm not good enough for the military, sir."

"Bull Shit! You are my boy! I chose you! Get your clothes together, take a shower, and come with me. You're going to serve in the army!"

I moved to the military base and decided to go all the way. I trained to become a paratrooper, and it was torture. My body wasn't ready for such rough military exercises, but my mind was. Workouts were rigorous and almost equal to my duties since Sergeant Alessandro had put himself in charge. When he'd seen me return, he screamed, "I'm going to make your life hell!"

And, he did. He made me his prey. He amplified my duties, above and beyond everyone else's. I cleaned toilets seven days a week under the thunderous roar of Alessandro's taunts and orders. If someone was sick, I had to replace them. My exhaustion was unbearable, but Alessandro wouldn't let that stop him. I needed rest like the other recruits, but he wouldn't allow it. Almost every night, in the middle of the night, he'd wake me up and put me to work. Some nights, he'd kick me awake, screaming, "Get your flabby ass in the latrines, boy! You don't have any right to be in the army other than to clean real soldiers' toilets!" Then, during exercises, he'd scream, "You're just a nigger, and I won't stop until you're out of here!"

Toiling with endless chores under Alessandro's criticisms while he delighted in mocking my slender frame and ugly face, every duty became a test of my resilience and a battle of wills, until my spirit was so bruised that I almost broke. I'd just entered high school at nineteen and felt I couldn't survive. My physical and mental faculties were stretched to the breaking point.

Alessandro. School. Army drills. Scrubbing duties. Degradation. Alessandro. Latrines. Humiliation. Studying. Alessandro. Homework. Sleep deprivation dragged me into the weeds.

If I lay down, I'd toss and turn, knowing Alessandro would show up at any minute. I was trapped in an embarrassing state of perpetual wakefulness. Hours stretched into eternity. I grew desperate amongst a gnawing hunger for sleep that wouldn't be fulfilled. I contemplated running from the army, then thought, "To tolerate or not to tolerate? That's my life question."

Here's a divergence:

I'd just been introduced to Shakespeare. I didn't want to just be. I wanted deliverance from the anguish and the wisdom to know what to tolerate. So, I asked myself how I had escaped two rape attempts, endured selling on the streets at age seven, and survived Dad for  three years. I had kept going, following God's bread crumbs. If one potential ice cream buyer said 'no,' I kept going because I'd decided to make that sale. When I was starving, I punched it up a notch by shining shoes. Maybe I met many demons, but the one or two saints were worth it. Good appeared once I'd made up my mind.

I continued my inner reflection, reminding myself I wouldn't become a loser like my father. I wouldn't turn to alcohol as an excuse to give up on life and pass on a hellish death wish to my child. I had to make choices like I did on the streets. Some people are so attuned to childhood abuse, humiliation, and degradation that they become accustomed to it and pass it on. The streets taught me not to do that. So, when I was nineteen and being called a 'nigger' by Sergeant Alessandro, screamed at for not being good enough for the army, singled out as the only non-rotating recruit, and woken up each night for whatever abuse he could devise, I would tell myself, "I chose the army to create a better life. I'm staying." I wouldn't surrender. I'd suffer through it and then prove my worth.

Here's a loving side-step:

Elaine and I had a son, Andrew, halfway through my two-year army stint. I was so excited and happy to feel alone no longer. I had someone to care for, and I'd never let him down; he was my saving grace because I discovered what unconditional love meant.

When it was time to jump from the airplane, I was one of the best in my squad. I had become rugged and had built biceps, quadriceps, hamstrings, glutes, and calves. My abs and glutes kept my pants up. Every muscle in my body had changed, and people told me it with their stares. But I'd been so focused on improving my life that I'd barely written to my family back in Goiás and hadn't seen them in nearly five years.

PHOTO: After a Year in the Military

9

Wearing My Sunday Best

I decided that spending my two-week vacation in Goiás was the best use of the only vacation I'd ever had. My family didn't know I had entered the army, and I wondered if they'd recognize me.

I hopped on a twenty-three-hour bus ride to Trindade, about five miles from Mom's house. I got a little motel room, ironed my uniform, and changed into it. I could have walked to Mom's house, and that's what she'd expect since I only walked everywhere as a child.

I wasn't about to walk. I would be impeccable and arrive in style, taking the best taxi available. I found a shiny, white, four-door sedan taxi and hired the driver. I explained that I wanted to make the best impression possible and asked the driver to stop in front of the house and honk the horn.

He slammed the horn with double punches. Nothing happened. "Do it again, do it again, please," I urged, my heart thumping. He honked it again, mashing it until I thought his hand would rupture the padding, and the neighborhood would protest in alarm. Nothing happened. The world just sat there, unimpressed.

"Keep going," I said. After several more double beeps, my little, platinum blond half-sister, Marcilene, peeked her head through the living room curtains. Her twelve-year-old face questioned, "What's that nice car doing here? Who is in that expensive car?"

I stepped from the car, waving and yelling, "Hello! Hello!" She burst into high-pitched screams that you'd expect from a kid who just saw Santa Claus coming down the chimney.

Please note:
Of course, no one in my family had ever seen Santa.

"It's Willian! It's Willian!" she exclaimed, running from the house and jumping on me, adding, "You're beautiful!"

I was surprised to see sincerely interested neighbors file out, one by one, until they were all in the middle of the street saying things like, "Wow! Wow! It's her son! He's back and look at him!"

While I was hugging my crying mother, one yelled, "Where have you been? Are you a policeman?"

"I'm a paratrooper for the military." My mom's tears fell even harder because I was the only person on both sides of my family to ever serve in the military.

"You look so different!" the crowd yelled.

My family and I went inside, where I told them about my life in Rio, and listened to how Mom had been coping with only the help of Marcilene. After a while, I finally confessed my secret urge- the one whispering for me to slip into the Presbyterian Church where I used to live and shake up the congregation like I had when I showed up at Mom's.

"I'm going to do the same thing I did with you, but in the middle of church service. I want those grown teenagers to see me!"

So, a couple of days later, I hired the same taxi and dressed in my freshly ironed uniform. I headed for church at a time that would put me there during the heart of the sermon. The taxi stayed outside while I went inside for worship.

A wave of memories crashed over me: the faces of my tormentors, the humiliation created by my attire and dirty skin, and the taunts by grown-ups such as Concella when I was just a kid. The past cruelty wanted to well up in my heart, but I wouldn't let it. I had begun to taste the likes of what dignity actually was, and it had started to be embedded under my skin.

I put my hat under my arm, walked into the church, and strolled slowly down the aisle with my head held high, eyes focused straight ahead, as the bishop spoke. My deliberate steps made sure everyone noticed. I made it to the front seat, in front of the bishop. He didn't recognize me.

After a bit of time, I looked to the right. Dropped jaws and wide-eyed astonishment stared back at me. "Is that really Willian?" their faces asked. I looked left. A stunned silence fell on their faces, where once laughter and ridicule lived. They looked like they'd seen a ghost. I mouthed, "Hello," and a hell-fire fear gaped back. A chorus of "No way!" was yelled back.

A woman pointed me out to the bishop, and he identified me. "We have a special guest," he told the congregation before asking me to stand. "It's Willian Lima," he kindly announced.

I rose, and then, I saw her- the blond bombshell, Concella, who'd called me a nigger and a monster, and all hell broke loose. How she hid her eyes, anxiously grated her nails on her Bible, and whispered to herself made it clear she was thinking irrational thoughts. Everyone around her began rustling louder until they spoke over the bishop and his sermon. Nervousness and commotion abounded until the service was stopped. A few churchgoers came to hug me.

"We have to get back to service!" the bishop railed, but it was hard for the congregation to keep their comments to themselves.

"You look so different," one said.

"I hope it's in a good way," I replied.

The bishop demanded that service resume, and after it was over, I got, "You look marvelous. Is that a police officer's uniform?" along with dozens of hugs.

"No. It's an elite service army uniform," I said, recalling my adolescent prayers that ensured God I'd buy nice church clothes if he gave me a way of making money and feeding my family.

I bathed in the energy of a rippling awe that cascaded outward from the congregation and seemed to have a warm glow. I had the effect I'd come for. Gone was the humiliated kid, the target of scorn, replaced by the power of self-acceptance. Gone was the shame, replaced by resilience. I extended my hand with forgiveness, acknowledging the past and letting go of it so our futures would be filled with hope and healing.

10

A Blessing in Disguise

After two grueling years in the military, enduring relentless harassment from Sergeant Alessandro, the government slashed military funding and terminated my position. Staring at the abrupt end of my military career, I couldn't fathom returning to the ghetto; I had come too far. My determination surged, realizing I had to soldier on, not just for myself, but to lift my son and Elaine out of their poverty-stricken neighborhood and secure a better life for my mother.

Thrown into shock and uncertainty, I grappled with the reality of my limited options. Elaine's family didn't have room for me in their home. I couldn't afford a place for us. I felt adrift with no high school diploma and a skill set confined to military duties, stocking video store shelves, and peddling goods on the streets.

Fortunately, my friend Rodrigo, also a casualty of military cutbacks, offered me a place to stay at his parents' house, promising mutual support in our job hunt. Reluctantly, I accepted his offer and landed a position at a supermarket a month later.

While stocking shelves wasn't my dream career, I couldn't afford to be picky. Yet, my conscience nagged at me as I struggled to make ends meet and provide adequate rent for Rodrigo's family. Determined to improve my situation, I embarked on a relentless job hunt, even if it meant sacrificing my pursuit of education by dropping out of high school altogether.

In a stroke of unexpected fortune, Rodrigo's aunt Clara, who worked at a private university, extended a lifeline by allowing me to submit my resume to her institution. Miraculously, despite my lack of experience and formal education, two months later, I received a call for an interview. The interview concluded with a simple yet promising statement: "We'll be in touch if we have something for you."

For the next three months, I continued to toil away at the supermarket, awaiting word from the university. Then, just when hope seemed fleeting, the call came. A secretarial job was mine for the taking. Though my heart raced with excitement, a lingering worry gnawed at me: did I possess the bookkeeping skills required for the role, or would I hopefully only be answering phones?

I was surprised to be given a desk and computer on my first day. A lead secretary sat with me, teaching me how their systems worked. A supervisor came in and taught me more. Before I knew it, I was an expert secretary, and after a year, the university found me a place to finish high school and paid for it.

I finished quickly and wanted to be a university student, knowing that tuition would be free for their professional courses since I was an employee. I took a national exam, passed it, and was accepted into their journalism college.

On weekdays, I had morning classes and worked from 1:00 to 11:00 pm. It was challenging, and I was embarrassed for still not having enough income to help my unemployed friend, Rodrigo. I convinced him to give me his resume, and before we knew it, he was working alongside me as a secretary and was studying for free. Somehow, I felt this was compensation for living in his home. I had one more little thing to be proud of: I helped a friend.

Feeling terribly embarrassed about being unable to help Rodrigo's family further, I took a risk and told them, "Thank you for all of your help and support, but it's time for me to move out." I moved into a university dormitory for student workers, where I'd have rent and multiple utility bills to pay. I had to keep pushing for more money because there was no way I'd have enough to live on and support my son.

I did some soul-searching. Through grounding myself and asking myself the hard questions, it dawned on me that meeting people may have been my most significant skill set. It was how I survived as a child, by sensing energy, reading faces, and knowing when to smile or stay silent. Connection was my currency. It had opened doors and shifted my fate. So, I hit Ipanema Beach and met as many people as possible. Soon, a man taught me massage therapy so I could work at their beach facilities on weekends.

"Great! That will increase my income. Thank God," I said, so happy that someone who barely knew me would help me.

"You'll get to meet people from all over the world," he responded.

My dream life was in full view. Andrew and Elaine would be out of the ghetto. I'd give Mom a better life by giving her things that Dad and my stepfather never could. I'd help my siblings. I'd live a life of dignity, never be involved with filthy vices, and be proud of myself.

My schedule was packed, and I didn't have time to study or do homework, yet getting good grades would be the only way to escape poverty fully. I had the energy to run a hectic schedule because I had a target: getting my family out of destitution. Having this energy told me that I was going in the right direction.

On the beach, I met people from all over, especially Europe and America. My military beach body often attracted them, and they frequently said, "You should be a model." But I didn't have time for that, and no matter how much I'd changed, the childhood shame made me believe modeling was an impossibility- only a place to get more degradation hurled at me.

I was uncomfortable that I couldn't speak my new friends' languages, so I bought English, Spanish, and French books. Soon, I had many new friends who would call me before visiting Brazil to plan times to spend together. I thank God for that because one of those friends, Peter, would later do me a favor that changed my life in ways I hadn't dreamed of. He said, "Willian, I will help you to be more successful. Just let me know what to do."

11

My Salt of the Earth

Nearing the end of my journalism studies at age twenty-five, I got a call from Valdenir. "Willian, Josemir has cancer, something like leukemia. He has bumps the size of baseballs all over his neck. He's in the hospital, very sick, and we don't know if he'll make it. You should come here as quickly as possible."

Without delay, I packed and went to the bus station because a plane ticket would have been way out of my budget. I arrived the following evening, desperately wanting to go straight to the hospital. But visiting hours were over.

I headed to the hospital the moment I awoke, where I found my brother with tubes coming out of his mouth. I introduced myself to his nurse and doctor, and they left the room. I turned to Josemir and watched him take one breath, then his machine went wonky, and Josemir's chest stopped moving. I beeped the nurse and said something was wrong. "His machine is acting weird."

She immediately returned, took one look at my brother, and said, "He just died right now." Josemir was in his early thirties, with a wife and three young kids.

My heart and brain went black. I couldn't feel or think a single thing. I hadn't seen my brother in ten years because he'd stayed in the city that Mom sent him to the last time we were split up. He was too far away for me to visit when I visited Mom. I believed I'd get a chance to see him again.

Just two weeks before his death, I had spoken with him. He didn't tell me he had cancer. I'm told that he didn't know. He had said, "I really want to see you, brother. I'd love to see you! When do you think you'll come to the center of Brazil and see your brother?"

I repeated that phone conversation in my head incessantly. It was the only thing that came to mind. Plunged into the depths of shock and unable to comprehend the scale of the loss, numbness drowned me. My perception was blurred, and my breathing became shallow gasps. "I should have done better. I should have seen him alive one last time," I cried. I clutched my heart, and my world voided until a light flickered, reminding me that I had to tell Mom that her son had just perished.

It couldn't happen again. I couldn't let my mother fall into the despair she had after losing her husband. I had to extinguish my fiery affliction and the one she was about to experience. I had to douse myself with something to be unrecognizable and no part of Mom's suffering. So much trauma surged through my veins that not a single cell of my being felt useful in this brutal circumstance.

I called Valdenir and said, "He just died. I am lost. Please tell Mom." Torturous screaming from many mouths was all I heard through the phone. This was the most brutal death of all. I didn't want to feel my feelings; they were too much. I loved my brother and had missed him for so long. "How could I arrive late? Why didn't I use my savings for a plane ticket?" I questioned myself, as the wailing continued.

"What do we do, Willian?" Valdenir asked. "We don't have money for a funeral or burial."

My mind and body were jolted by an impulse and awareness: poor people didn't get genuine funerals and burials. If we couldn't afford a burial, the government only allowed a body to have a grave for up to two years, sometimes only one, before replacing it with another.

My brother deserved respect, and I had a little money saved for my future or an emergency, whichever came first. The latter always came first in my family, so I began to feel absurd for even believing in a future.

I called for a mortician to transfer and prepare Josemir's body, and I rode in the hearse. At the funeral home, the man told me to pick a coffin. The cheapest and weakest one was all I could afford. "My brother deserves an honorable burial," I kept telling myself, in astonishment at how expensive dying was.

I watched the man clean up my brother's body, extract liquid from him, and stuff cotton deep inside. "I don't want to see this!" I yelled after it was too late. I had been in a sort of stupor, but then jolted into the trauma I'd been incurring. "I feel dizzy. Can I get out of here?" And, of course, the mortician said yes.

I went to Josemir's house to fetch a suit. When I returned, the mortician had me dress my brother in it and put makeup on his face. I don't know where the strength came from to do that, except I was glad Mom didn't have to.

I had only a trivial amount of money left, and I knew it would go to purchasing land for his burial. So, there wouldn't be a church or a funeral-home funeral. I rode in the hearse to my sister's home, finding my family in tears, and Momma fixed in a gaze that seemed to say she had been betrayed. When the coffin was brought inside, she said nothing. She stared at her son, stroking his face and hair for hours. Everyone stayed overnight, saying their goodbyes.

The next day, we took Josemir to the cemetery, where I bought land for him to rest in for eternity. I punished myself, and at that moment, it seemed rightfully so. I only thought, "Willian, you could have gotten here sooner. You could have flown and seen your brother alive. You could have gotten here much quicker and done better!" I was in severe mourning and self-reprimand.

Here's a climactic ending to this life chapter: Dreams started. Josemir was in every one of them every night. At first, I thought it was because I was mourning him, but the dreams got more real, more active, as if I were with him upon awakening. In the last one, he sat across from me in my bed and said, "Willian, everything is okay. I'm in a  good place. I appreciate everything you did for me when I died." When I awoke, it was as if he were still with me. I felt I'd just touched him. It was more real than this supposed reality. I knew it was genuine, felt better, and moved on.

I returned to Rio, where I was diagnosed with cancer months later. I needed surgery and months of treatment. With the best surgeons and therapies hours away in São Paulo and the necessity to stay near work, I was at a complete loss. Here's a summation of Rio de Janeiro's health care: it was hell on earth. It might have taken a year to get my surgery. Cancer treatments were subpar at best, doctors and staff were inadequately trained, and the system was fraught with corruption.

Knowing my bank account would be drained dry, I had to get to São Paulo. Fortunately, my friends in the city offered to let me stay at their home. This moment underscored the power of building bridges. The surgery and recovery were dreadful, and without my friends, my only option would have been treatment in Rio, which promised a more extended, more grueling recovery period, if there was any recovery at all.

The university granted me time off until I recovered. I called Valdenir, and she met me in São Paulo to help me through the excruciating recovery that left me diminished. The cancer, surgery, and treatments ravaged my body. I lost muscle, grew weak, and returned to a scrawny version of myself.

Here are my final thoughts on the matter: Perhaps the fatality rate of the Cesium-137 incident was higher than they officially reported.

12

It Came to Light

Returning to Rio, I was back to full-time studying and working, but I wasn't the same. My muscles and strength were gone, so I tried to recover my body by adding gym workouts to my full schedule. I started to get fit again.

It took some time, yet I began receiving familiar advice I'd heard before having cancer. People said to take up modeling. "I don't have time," I'd say. They'd usually respond with something like, "At least try. Go to a modeling agency. With your sculpted body, you should be a model."

I thought they were right in at least one area. If I didn't try, I wouldn't know if it was possible. So I applied at one modeling agency, then another, and another. "No. You're not good for us," I'd get repeatedly, with hints that they didn't like my skin's dark tone.

After much searching, I found an agency that hired dark-skinned people. Soon, my arm was in a magazine, and I was a behind-the-scenes extra in commercials. But there was a thorn in my side. The agency kept charging me for taking more and more pictures to place in my modeling book, and spending that money took away from more important areas of my life. After months of getting zero significant jobs, only ones where I'd walk behind their White stars, I questioned my decision to try modeling.

When I approached managers with my concerns, I was told to keep going because soon a Novela would lift me into greater roles. Novelas are daytime Brazilian drama shows, not too different from America's soap operas. However, they are so influential that they shape fashion, music, public opinion, and even politics. The possibility of landing a role on a Novela renewed my excitement for modeling. A Novela could help me make extra money for Andrew and Mom. Plus, the idea of being seen inside one of those brightly lit boxes, instead of having a door slammed in my face, lit something in me. It felt like hope. So I kept showing up, chasing that shimmer of possibility.

Yet, the deeper I dug, the more I saw the limits of what they saw in me. Novelas hired me, but they pushed me to the sidelines- backstage, out of frame, always just out of reach. I wasn't acting; I was a placeholder. My time meant more than that. I could either waste it waiting to be seen or invest it in something real. I chose education and good, honest work over the bright lights.

Life started lighting up in other ways. My university co-worker, Maria, began talking about her mother and friend moving to Spain for work, and that they made more money in Europe. "Wow! It would be amazing to see another country," I'd think while she talked, and wonder if better money-making opportunities existed for me in Spain.

One day, Maria came to work, grabbed me, and said, "You can go to Spain and live at my mother's home for a little while. You'd have to help Mom with expenses, though." I called Peter, and he bought me a plane ticket. I got a passport and abruptly finished my journalism course by diving into much research and writing a thesis. The next thing I knew, I was living in the beautiful city of Valencia, Spain.

Spain was an unimaginably new world, with its signs I couldn't read, places I couldn't find, and people moving too fast for me to catch up. I realized how Momma must have seen the world her entire life.

Naturally, Maria's mom expected me to start paying rent quickly. With just a few Spanish words tucked under my belt, navigating life in Spain was a real challenge. But I did not let that sway me. I kept positivity in my mind: "I'll give it everything I've got and regret will never live in my heart."

I walked all over town, getting lost because so many things looked similar. After two weeks, I walked into a lounge and told the owner, "I am from Brazil and am looking for a job."

"Come back tomorrow," he said, "You can wait tables, organize, and clean. I'll see you tomorrow."

For a stranger to trust and hire me on the spot was an unexpected blessing. Yet, it's what the world could use more of: people whose faith in the good runs so deep that they extend blessings without pause. I took it as a breadcrumb that I was in the right place and to simply do my best.

Since it was a summertime lounge, I wouldn't have a year-round job, but it was an opportunity to turn another one of life's corners. Who knew where it would lead? To being able to scrape by? Having an apartment of my own? Alien streets? A couple of hookers with an empty room? A church with an empty bed? A ghetto, or a surprise I had never imagined? I didn't have my sights on a prize or the end of the road; I had them on the goodness of the moment, so I'd be aware of more good when it appeared.

I worked at the lounge and slept at the couple's house for two months, after which I began feeling they were uncomfortable with my presence. I told my boss, and he gave me an extra job working around the clock to receive supplies. I slept in the lounge, working day and night, but I didn't have rent to pay. I had food and water, so I thrived.

After several months, I got to know Gema, the lounge singer. We hit it off and were quickly in a good relationship. We went on a date at the beach, where I wore my yellow and green Brazilian swimsuit. Walking to the water, a strange man passed us, glaring at us like he knew something we didn't. I was relieved when he got far enough away that I couldn't feel his eyes, but then he turned. He looked directly at me, leaned forward like he was about to charge, his expression seeming to suck the air from atop the ocean, and then relaxed his extra inquisitive eye. Being very uncomfortable, I almost bolted when he scanned every inch of my body.

"What is this guy doing looking at me like that?" I asked Gema. "Is this normal?"

"This is not normal, Willian. That guy wants something from you," she responded.

I tried my best to divert my attention from him, but my spine tingled like an unknown energy was on me, frightening or not, I wasn't sure. After a couple of minutes, he came over.

"Sorry for checking out your body. I am Manuel. What's your name?"

"Why do you want to know?"

"I'm not flirting. You have the exact profile that my modeling agency is looking for. You're exotic, and everything about you is wonderful. Where are you from?"

"I am Willian Lima, and I'm from Brazil."

"Oh, Brazil. That's the reason you are wearing green and yellow trunks."

"Yes."

"Here's my card. If you're interested, go to my agency tomorrow to take a couple of pictures and see what happens. We need people like you. You'd be a new and wonderful face!"

After Manuel left, I was very suspicious, expecting that if this modeling studio accepted me, I'd get the same results as I did back in Brazil. "What do you think, Gema?"

"Maybe it's true. Maybe it's not. How will you know if you don't go and check it out?" was Gema's advice.

I went the next day with my swimsuit in hand, as Manuel had instructed. I gave his card to a lady receiving applicants and told her about what happened the day before.

"I want to introduce you to our supervisor," she replied, and walked me to another woman who scanned me from toes to hair, as if exploring how big a question mark I was.

"I want to see you in your bathing suit," the second woman said.

After I changed, they told me to stand in front of a white wall and began taking pictures from every angle, from a distance and up close. Cameras flashed, capturing every awkward, self-conscious grimace. I understood how a deer must feel when caught in headlights- except the deer wasn't half-naked.

"We're seeing if you are photogenic, and we'll get back to you as soon as we have something for you."

I left, saying to myself, "This will never work."

13

Manna from Heaven

After a week and a great show of support from my boss at the lounge, I received a call. "This is the Richy Maroe Agency. Is this Willian Lima?"

"Yes."

"Are you interested in runway fashion modeling? Several fashion stylists have seen your pictures and are interested in you walking the catwalk for them. Are you willing?"

"Yes, of course. I'm interested."

"Then, please come back to our agency to meet them tomorrow. You'll have to dress in their clothes to see if you're a good fit. Valencia Fashion Week starts next week. Have you ever walked a runway?"

Here's a long detour: I walked a runway one time in 2003. The pageant was titled "Men's Black Beauty," and I participated to determine if I deserved the title of Model.

Although people told me I had a lovely face and body, I didn't believe it. My confidence had been on the ground since the teenagers at that Presbyterian church told me I was ugly, and Concella buried it when she called me a monster, to name one affront. It didn't matter how many people told me I was worthy and supported me; I had to prove it to myself.

In those days, models were predominantly White. It wouldn't be until 2009 that São Paulo Fashion Week would impose a quota of ten percent Black or Indigenous models. I always felt inferior. That runway was tiny and a place where I didn't feel worthy. I had internalized the childhood bullying and taken it with me into adulthood. I walked the catwalk anyway and took second place. It gave me a new confidence that spilled over into other parts of my life. I knew I could do more than the little I'd done.

"Valencia Fashion Week is crucial to fashion in Spain. You'd be a new face, and if you do well, we'll get you more work," the woman continued.

At least three of the many designers at the Richy studio the next day chose me to model their brands. But first, I'd have to learn to walk the big catwalk properly. "Our designers want you to walk the runway in a special way. You'll need to act, smile properly, keep your eyes forward, and show the clothes the proper way to sell them," they explained, sending me to an enormous runway with a trainer.

The trainers said I was a natural and seemed familiar with the runway. I thought, "Yeah, I think I practiced in a church back in Brazil." I prepared in designer clothes while they instructed and took pictures, and then I went back to my routine at the lounge.

On the first day of Valencia Fashion Week, I stepped out into the bustling squares and thoroughfares, nervous to put my face out there for others to see. A whirlwind of sights and sounds blasted my senses, and the importance of this event to Spain's third-largest city was visible in the pace and on the faces of the town. But amidst the chaos, a sight stopped me dead in my tracks. A larger-than-life billboard, advertising the show, towered over the square. In disbelief, I blinked my eyes, thinking I was in a dream and that I couldn't possibly be staring at my own face.

Time stood still as my heart thumped up ten notches in a steady rhythm of excitement and doubt. I was almost embarrassed that others might know it was me, and hoped they weren't looking. I turned left, proceeding by a newspaper stand where my face was plastered on the covers. Then I turned right, almost rushing to the biggest day of my life outside Andrew's birth. My expectations of myself had just been kicked up, walking past sighting after sighting of my face.

For the remainder of my stride to the venue, I focused on my gratitude for being there, for everyone who helped me get there, and for my journey through tolerance that kept me going until that very moment that I was the male face of a major fashion event for Spanish designers.

I prayed, "Please, God, don't let me fudge up."

14

My Seventh Heaven

My first stride out of the gate filled me with apprehension. "Will I mess up? Will they think I'm ugly? Am I worthy of this?" Knowing now not to believe every thought that flashed through my mind and that those thoughts were what Concella and Alessandro would have me think, I turned them into fuel for my fire. My nerves shot one by one, some in nervous anticipation of doom and others in an overwhelming play of excitement.

Wearing a multi-colored mankini and jacket that left little to the imagination, I was inspired by a heat that welled up through my spine and seemed to seep from my pores. I took one step and then gracefully strode, my eyes locked straight forward, my mind shutting out the room.

I felt the audience's gaze. It lifted me, propelling me into a confidence that allowed my body to move in a symphony of fluidity and poise. At the end of the runway, I paused with a smoldering gaze, allowing the room to behold me in those designer clothes. Designer clothes! I turned as a tear wanted to brim, but I wouldn't let it, for I had to change clothes to do the catwalk again and again.

At the end of Valencia Fashion Week's first day, I was intoxicated by life and the universal grace that had put people near me to discover my potential. The following day, I headed to the square that would be replaying the first night's show on television. Again, I couldn't believe my eyes when I appeared on the big screen. The camera scanned my body. A spotlight caught my physique, casting a golden light around my dark, bronze skin that seemed to illuminate the runway. I felt I was in a dream. My body was sculpted almost to perfection, and the audience breathed me in.

"Is that you?" I heard. I humbly smiled, not believing this moment was happening, shook people's hands, and said, "Yes, that's me." A crowd packed in around me. Women took paper and pens from their purses, and others snapped photos. "Can I have a photo with you? Can I have your autograph?" many watchers asked.

I returned to that runway over thirty times that week, then returned to my job at the lounge. I was utterly astounded when customers recognized me, and my hand became sore from signing so many autographs. I felt like an instant celebrity. It was a little odd because, for much of my twenty-seven years, being noticed was traumatizing. But this newfound recognition had benefits. More fashion designers saw my face and called the Richy Agency. "He's exotic and the new face of the show from Brazil," they'd tell their customers.

The next thing I knew, fashion designers across Spain wanted me in their shows. I modeled for fashion weeks in captivating Madrid, where charm and passion pulsate through its streets, culture, and people. I headed for Barcelona, where flowers cascaded from windows down to their twisting stone paths, Palma, Majorca, and Jaén. In Jaén, I closed my first runway show, turned more heads, and started making serious cash.

I told my lounge boss the shocking news that my modeling career had just gone big. He said, "No problem, Willian. This is a huge opportunity for you. You should do modeling. I'd think you were a loser if you didn't."

"Thank you, boss," I replied, processing that word I'd been running from my entire life- 'loser.'

"I'll always have a job for you if you need one," he said, adding what so many other people had told me: "Go and don't look back."

I responded the way I did to my inner voice. "I'll always look back at the people who supported me and did such nice things that I made it here today."

I moved into an apartment building housing models from other countries, where I was finally a part of a community. The models felt like my family for the next two years as I was called to fashion shows across Europe: Paris to Lisbon, London to Copenhagen, and Milan to Berlin. By age twenty-nine, I had modeled for major designers such as Valentino and Yves Saint Laurent, and walked the runways in seven countries and twenty European cities.

Who needs a self-help book when life itself reveals such raw beauty, and God sends miracles disguised as strangers?

PHOTO: Willian's First European Catwalk

15

An Act of God

After two years in Europe, I was on the brink of true wealth, poised to lift my son out of the ghetto, buy Mom a home, and finally break free from the relentless struggle of providing for my family. However, my absence had taken its toll- Andrew barely remembered my face except through photos his mother showed him, and the ache of missing him consumed me.

The promise of prosperity for my family and the commitment to being a loving, present father waged a fierce battle in my heart. I was at a psychological crossroads, torn between two powerful desires every single day. Ultimately, the wealth of love for my son won out. I had saved enough to make a significant difference, so I ended my European career and returned to Rio.

I promised Andrew I'd never leave him again and assured him of a better home as we hugged and cried. I then set off for Goiás to surprise Mom.

Upon arriving, I was hit with a harsh reality: Mom and my half-sister had been evicted from their home, claimed by my deceased stepfather's family. My stepbrother had kicked them out. These bitter discoveries overshadowed the joy of reunion, but my resolve to be there for my family was stronger than ever.

No one knew where Mom and Marcilene had gone, but the rumor was that their new home was hours away. After much investigation, I discovered that the rumor was true and found Mom's address.

Squalor– that's what I found Mom living in. Her life had sunk to tragic depths, and I was devastated. Her home was two small rooms covered by mud and corrugated metal. There was no bathroom. At least my stepfather's home had a toilet. Her new toilet was a hole in the ground in the woods behind a gate, which was her make-believe privacy wall. She had one piece of furniture– a sofa with a hole the size of a basketball. The kitchen had a small cabinet, a spot for a makeshift stove, and a refrigerator– neither of which Mom owned. She slept on a slab of something unidentifiable, and her shower room was covered with black plastic for privacy since walls didn't exist there.

Whatever my mother was living in, I couldn't call it a house. It was a heartbreaking scene, a stark reminder of how far she had fallen and how urgent it was to bring her some semblance of dignity and comfort. So, I set out to live a dream I'd had most of my life: I would buy Mom a home.

Willian's Mother's Home

Without telling her, I found a house for sale- the nicest one in her community- so she could stay near my half-sister. I decided that I'd do my best to buy that home. After several weeks, I bought it, did some conniving, and then asked Mom out for a walk. She agreed, and when we passed that house, I said, "The government is giving land to people who can't afford to own homes, and people are building nice houses now. Look at that one there, Mom."

"Oh, that's very nice," Mom replied.

"One day, who knows, Mom, maybe we'll win the lottery."

"Yeah, right," she said.

"Tell me everything that happened in your life while I was in Europe, Mom," I inquired, leading Mom to the farthest end of the neighborhood while she told her story.

"Let's go back. I'm tired of walking," I concluded, and ushered her back to that house after a nice stroll. I had her stop to take a closer look. "This house is really nice, Mom. Unfortunately, we can't afford it, but it sure would be nice for you."

"I would absolutely love it!" Mom said. "It would be perfect because it's not easy where I live. But I'm happy since I don't worry about paying rent. I can't complain."

"You're right, Mom. You don't need to complain about anything because here, take these," I said, handing her the keys.

"What are these for?"

"We stopped here because I bought you this house."

"No! No! No! No! No! No! You're kidding, right?"

"It's yours, Mom," I said, kissing her on the cheek.

"You can't be serious. You are joking with me, right?"

"No, Mom. It's not a joke. This is your house!"

Cradling her head with her hands, Mom cried, "Oh my God!" We hugged and cried repeatedly as she screamed, "Oh my God!"

We unlocked the door and went inside, where I had the glorious moment of showing her everything I'd bought for her. Here's the list: refrigerator, beds, cabinets, sofa, television, and washing machine. I'd also stocked the kitchen with food. I showed her the second bedroom, saying, "This is mine when I visit."

I finally deemed myself a man of worth because I'd given my mother dignity. She moved into her new home the same day, and after two months of assisting Mom, I returned to Rio with a slimmer bank account. I headed straight to the modeling agencies to tell them of my successes in Europe and share my pictures. But still, they wouldn't hire me. None of them.

Although I promised Andrew I wouldn't leave, modeling opportunities led me to Panama, where I'd make enough money to continue to support my family. I promised Andrew we'd talk almost daily, and we did during my two years there, where I modeled with the stunning actress Patricia Velásquez from *The Mummy*.

Missing Andrew again, I arrived at the same crossroads I had a few years prior. This time, I didn't struggle over it; I just went home. I returned to massage therapy on the beach, where I'd see my American and European friends. Many of them had apartments in Brazil, and some gave me real estate jobs to help them get rental occupants, collect rent, fix things, and clean. They offered me those jobs so I could stay close to my son.

Soon, there were surprising benefits. One apartment owner was friends with the American actress Rosario Dawson from *Sin City*, *Marvel* series, such as *The Defenders*, and numerous big-screen movies. We met on New Year's Eve and became friends, and she asked me to attend *The Black-Eyed Peas* concert with her that night on Copacabana Beach. Rosario was good friends with *The Black-Eyed Peas*' star, Fergie, so I was allowed to stay backstage with band member Will. I. Am.

After the concert, the fans were going wild, and fireworks echoed across the sky, crossing the nearly three million people who had gathered on the beach. The sand beneath our feet felt like a second heartbeat to get us on our way, but hordes of people crashed in, making it unsafe for us to get to the parking lot. But we had to make it to the Copacabana Palace- an iconic Rio de Janeiro hotel known for its grandeur. So, security formed a human tube all the way to the parking lot to protect us.

Fergie yelled, "Everyone needs to hold hands!"

I grabbed Rosario's hand with one hand and Fergie's with the other. Burying our heads down in our chests to avoid getting hit by rowdy fans, we dashed through the human hallway, staring at the ground, and gripping each other tightly.

As we neared the limousine, something compelled me to look up- something not unlike that little voice in the gas station when I was nine. I raised my head. My eyes locked with another's. Straight ahead, in the row of guards lined up like army ants, I recognized the familiar figure staring at me. He was a former antagonist. My heart jolted, being eye-to-eye with that one particular security guard. A whirlwind of surprise and disbelief swirled inside me. The once nihilistic scorn that dressed that face had been replaced with a confusing air, one that said there may be something more to this thing called Life.

Sergeant Alessandro- correction, Security Guard Alessandro- tried to steady himself, but his jaw dropped, and panic flashed through his eyes.

"Willian!" Alessandro yelled in shock, then peered at Fergie and back to me with eyebrows shot up to the moon and a face seemingly caught fire by the sun.

I paused with a smile. A wave of energy washed over me like Christ the Redeemer touched me, and holy water had just cleansed my soul.

Of course, Fergie didn't know what was happening. She said, "Come on! Let's go!" while Alessandro was frozen with embarrassing discomfort.

"Bye-bye, Sarge!" I yelled and waved, knowing God had just washed my soul clean of every foul word, starving day, taunt, beating, bully, and rejection. I was dignified and free.

My Final Aside Worth Highly Noting: In 2013, Rio's population was around sixteen million. The New Year's Eve crowds on Copacabana Beach are typically 2 - 3 million people. The odds of crossing paths with one specific person, especially someone from the shadows of my past, were microscopic. And yet, while rushing through masses of people while holding the hands of two radiant celebrities, I felt the message to look up. I locked eyes with Sergeant Alessandro- the man who once tried to break me. The universe didn't just circle back. It spun full-force, knowing exactly where he'd be. God dropped me, shining and dignified in manners I'd never before imagined, right in front of my symbol of every antagonist in this human dream.

PHOTOS: Memorable Moments with Well-Known Figures

Willian and Rosario Dawson

Willian and Fergie

16

⟨❦⟩

Afterword

*-"..as long as you hear what is good and positive, as long as you want,
need, and welcome what is good and positive, you will
be able to maintain contact to God. You will experience the truth
in your own body and consequently will no longer be a person without
energy, but will be strengthened through God's power so that you
will have a positive attitude for the rest of your life."[1]*
Bruno Gröning
1906-1959
German Spiritual Healer

As it remains today, a positive mindset was one of Willian's most defining qualities, allowing him to see through life's trials and into its opportunities. It pushed him to leap toward hidden horizons, rebel against poverty, and search for unknown possibilities, even if the risks were great and the outcomes could have been far more dire.

His father denied life, apparent in alcoholism and abuse. Willian chose an alternate path to that grand denial; he chose life, where the greatest battles are not fought on the streets, but in the unseen arena of the soul. And although Willian felt something irreplaceable had been stolen at the hands of his father, he wanted the good in life enough to find it.

In the moment that burdens are too much for our hearts to carry, lies the crossroads of accepting despair as home or searching for what yearns to be restored. Willian labeled his search as one for dignity, while ancestral scarcity continued to weave through the fabric of his life. Surrendering to despair could have been the easier route. Yet, Willian wholeheartedly welcomed the good and chose it as the light to guide his path.

Uncannily, when this world steals a sacred inner nugget, we can't reclaim it from this world. That inherent abundance, love, and respect for Self and Life had not come from this world. When it's snatched, we are forced within and into a relationship with a creative force, which generates inner strength from deep within. If we turn that strength into love, we are already home. Then, if we discover what we love enough to make life worth understanding, somehow, through the search, that nugget is restored.

Willian found love in the idea of being educated and having long-term security for his family. Without this love, he could have succumbed to despair, as the only person who ever promised him the same was the government lady. She never returned.

A year before his spiritual purification on Copacabana Beach, Willian's fortitude was tested with his mother's stage three ovarian cancer. Willian marshaled every resource at his disposal in a desperate bid to beat the odds. Knowing treatment in Goiás would be a death sentence, he bought her a plane ticket to São Paulo, where she was admitted to his friend's cancer clinic, and lived with other friends, who opened their hearts and home to Willian and his mother.

Surgery and years of chemotherapy and radiation were prescribed. After a successful surgery and a two-month hospital stay, Willian's mother needed monthly trips for chemotherapy and radiation, but being illiterate, she couldn't do it alone. For five years, Willian bought monthly plane tickets for Valdenir and their mother to be shuttled back and forth the nearly 600 miles between Goiás and São Paulo. When his mother fully recovered, Willian recognized the result of his hard work: his mother's cancer-free life. This was one of the proudest days of his life.

Again, he visited the Presbyterian church in Goiás, where he found Concella in a deep emotional struggle. Her oldest child, the same age as Willian when he endured her cruel words, had mental disabilities. Also being Black in an all-White church, Concella's son was subjected to the same cruelties that his mother once inflicted on Willian. Yet, instead of apologizing to Willian, she stiffened, her face seemingly wrought with shame. Her gaze eerily lingered on Andrew, Willian's teenage son. Through a bizarre flicker of envy, her eyes dashing back and forth between the two boys, she did not extend an inner light, but masked her bitterness behind a polite smile.

Willian felt Concella was learning a lesson in the power of empathy to break cycles of darkness. He extended his hand and kindness to be a part of this change.

Willian's life illustrates that hiding from life does not build the good. Running from life doesn't allow us to discover the good in this third-dimensional world. His life shows that true strength cannot be measured by an abundance of strength or a lack of adversity, but by endurance in the face of it. And by doing so, the light we emit becomes reflected in our world.

Treasuring his connections, he desired to treat his friends with dignity by speaking their languages. In essence, he'd already taught himself Portuguese and later learned English, Spanish, and a little French, German, and Italian through reading books.

Willian was called to modeling gigs for Africa, more European cities, and in Central America, Cuba, and Colombia.

Although Willian has lifted his mother and every living sibling out of hopelessness, his father, sober for four years of this book's publishing in 2025, refuses help. He stays in misery as a sacrifice for the cruelty he inflicted on his children.

The eternal voice, resounding with self-love, grace, and trust, calls us to build its light, no matter how minuscule or indescribable it first seems. Because the moment we stop, we become trapped, entangled in the tightly wound memories of fear and doubt that the shadow has been weaving for generations. When we push through, when we move with the force within, we foster more of that light which tugs at the threads of torment and dissolves darkness. Momentum is one of our greatest salvations in this foreign land.

Michelle Faith Lucas

[1]Bruno Gröning, in a letter, per *An Introduction to the Teaching of Bruno Gröning*, Grete Häusler, 2008, 5th edition

PHOTO: Modeling Gig for Piaget Watches

PHOTOS: Momma's New Home

Front of Willian's Mother's New Home

Inside Willian's Mother's New Home

Pass It On Book Series

Y**our Journey Doesn't End Here...**

The Runway Runaway is the third of 144 books in the *Pass It On* series. Each story unlocks new insights and powerful lessons from life's most profound challenges. By sharing in the wisdom of others, you can find deeper understanding and renewed strength for your path. Check out these titles to be released in 2025 and don't miss our first box set of twelve, available during the 2025 holidays.

OUR HEARTSONG (Released Feb. 2025. Nonfiction/Spirituality/ Happiness) Journey into peace and the heart of life, which is unconditional love. This uplifting and inspiring book is a walk into profound truths discovered by the author, who lived in an I AM sanctuary for over a decade. (Wolfgang Werner)

WHISPERS FROM THE ANCIENT ONES (Released March 2025. Nonfiction/Self-Help on Abuse, Anger, and Forgiveness) If you could do one thing to transform your life, heal your emotions, and liberate yourself from the past, would you do it? That one life-changing tool exists within you. This book is a two-part guide, from the author's story of trauma to triumph to the life-changing tools that rewire the brain and release emotional wounds. (E.C. Sanders)

TRUCKIN' THROUGH TWO REALITIES - **(Fiction/Spirituality)** Heaven and Hell aren't places; they're patterns. Join a hilariously unfiltered schizophrenic truck driver on his quest to recover humanity's lost wisdom - armed only with the insights he refused to surrender during his terrible twos and his surprisingly spot-on interpretations of ancient scripture. (A.M. Wessel)

THE FIRST DIMENSION (IN EVERY SOUL IS A SONG – BOOK I) - (Nonfiction/Multi-dimensional Healing) Multi-dimensional healing and spiritual guidance rooted in the extraordinary clarity of a near-death experience - offering not just inspiration, but a soul-deep recalibration to uplift every aspect of life. This is a rare invitation to awaken inner truth, transcend limitation, and realign with the unseen forces that shape our reality. (Rev. M. Lucas)

CAPRIS-CORN - (Nonfiction/Self-Help/Astrology) Depicting the wisdom and karmic imprint of Capricorn in astrology, *Capris Corn* is Ezra the goat's remarkable journey to mastering fortune. If 'going it alone' defines much of your life, Capricorn likely rules your karma, and this tender, soulful tale will guide you to a freer path where peace of mind will lead you. (Rev. F. James)

ARIA - (Memoir) An opera singer's rebellious journey to finding her voice: From Mormonism to Namaste (Violet Sage)

www.ingramcontent.com/pod-product-compliance
Lightning Source LLC
Chambersburg PA
CBHW061705120626
46550CB00003B/1097